MW01110385

[ CODING YOUR PASSION™ ]

# USING COMPUTER SCIENCE IN
# MARKETING
# »CAREERS«

CARLA MOONEY

Rosen YA™
New York

Published in 2020 by The Rosen Publishing Group, Inc.
29 East 21st Street, New York, NY 10010

**Library of Congress Cataloging-in-Publication Data**

Names: Mooney, Carla, 1970– author.
Title: Using computer science in marketing careers / Carla Mooney.
Description: First edition. | New York : Rosen Publishing, 2020. | Series: Coding your passion | Includes bibliographical references and index.
Identifiers: LCCN 2018044925| ISBN 9781508187196 (library bound) | ISBN 9781508187189 (pbk.)
Subjects: LCSH: Marketing—Technological innovations. | Business enterprises—Computer networks. | Electronic commerce. | Computer science—Vocational guidance.
Classification: LCC HF5410 .M66 2020 | DDC 658.800285—dc23
LC record available at https://lccn.loc.gov/2018044925

*Manufactured in China*

# CONTENTS

# INTRODUCTION

Since 2011, Anna Soo has led the marketing operations team at Commvault, a data protection and information management software company in New Jersey. When she was hired, Soo became the first person at Commvault to focus on marketing operations. At first, she created marketing reports that the company was not able to easily produce. "We had a few marketing technology tools in place, but they weren't integrated, and marketers were doing a lot of things manually. It would take several hours each week to export the data, match the fields, generate our pivot tables before we even start to analyze the results," said Soo in an interview posted on Allocadia.com.

Since then, Soo's marketing operations team has grown to eight people, who work closely with other marketing professionals in the company. The team designs and implements technology solutions and builds processes to help the marketing department improve its efficiency and effectiveness. In a recent project, Soo's team integrated two software platforms used by the company—Allocadia for managing marketing costs and Workfront for managing project tasks. "We wanted to see if we could get the two connected together, which would reduce the amount of time our marketers spent inputting information," said Soo. "We set it up so that our marketers can

Automated marketing reports allow marketing professionals to efficiently analyze the status of marketing project tasks and their related costs.

create a line item in Allocadia for an activity they're planning—a field event, for example—and then just hit a single button to send that item to Workfront where it becomes a project. All the data fields are included, no manual entry needed." In future phases of the project, Soo's team plans to add more automated solutions for marketing's processes. "The goal of all these is the same: saving us time [and] manpower," said Soo.

Technology is changing the way people do business. For many years, a company's traditional business departments, such as marketing and accounting, operated independently of its technology department. When a marketing professional needed help building a web page or programming a report, he or she called a computer technology professional from the technology department. In recent years, the two fields have begun to overlap. As companies are increasingly using technology to make business processes more efficient, more business careers require professionals who have technical and coding skills. Digital marketing, marketing automation, e-commerce, and search engine optimization are just a few examples of areas within marketing that benefit from computer science and coding skills. By combining business and technical skills, marketing professionals can help companies improve efficiencies and increase profits.

The demand for marketers with digital and technical skills is creating new opportunities for people with an interest in computer science and marketing. Kavita Paliwal, a marketing analyst, writes in a LoginRadius blog post:

> **Marketing has evolved in the past few years, and if you have a look at modern online marketing, you will see that code is everywhere! There's code in your websites, email campaigns, and even your analytics campaign. Learning how to code will help you to collaborate with your customers as well as clients. Apart from that, you can create new ideas**

and campaigns that actually work! You don't need to become a developer, but a general understanding of coding is very useful in modern marketing where user experience is the first priority.

In marketing, there are many different career specialties students can pursue that use computer science. Companies employ digital marketers, e-commerce and search optimization specialists, marketing automation professionals, web designers and developers, and more. With so many opportunities, careers that merge marketing and computer science can fit many backgrounds and interests.

# CHAPTER ONE

# THE CHANGING WORLD OF MARKETING AND COMPUTER SCIENCE

Across the country, people see advertisements enticing them to buy products and services almost everywhere they look—in print, online, on television and radio, and even on their phones. They receive notifications about new products and upcoming sales through mailed catalogs and brochures or via emails or text messages. They take customer surveys, participate in store loyalty programs, and browse websites. All of these activities are designed, planned, and executed by marketing professionals.

Marketing is much more than creating a print or online ad. Marketing is the entire process of getting a product or service from a company to the consumer. This involves the research to create the product, identifying potential customers, setting prices, creating advertising and promotional campaigns, and many

Enormous advertising signs line New York's Times Square and compete with each other to attract the attention of potential customers as they pass through the area.

Overall, there are three main goals of marketing. First, marketing seeks to identify and capture the attention of a target market, the people most likely to want and need its product or service. Second, marketing tries to convince the consumer to buy the product or service, now and in the future. Third, marketing works to create an easy and cost-effective way to get the product or service to the customer. This includes deciding which products to stock in a store, how to display them within the store, and what promotions or sales to offer. All of

these decisions support marketing's overall goal—
to sell more products or services. As a result, many
companies spend enormous amounts of time and
money on marketing.

## THE FOUR P'S OF MARKETING

Marketing involves four elements, known as the
four *P*'s—product, price, promotion, and place.
Each element is part of a plan to effectively target
consumers. From the beginning, marketing is involved
with a product. Marketing departments test new
product ideas and designs with groups of customers
or through surveys. They determine if potential buyers
would be interested in the new product and what
styles, sizes, flavors, and scents they want the most.
They even test packaging designs with small groups of
customers to see which is the most appealing.

Price is often an important factor in a customer's
buying decision. If a product is priced too high, people
will not buy it. If priced too low, the company's profit
margin will drop. To determine how much customers
would be willing to pay, marketing professionals
research the price charged by their competitors for
similar products. For new products, they test different
prices with consumer groups.

Promotion is another important element of
marketing. Promotion involves the communication
tools a company uses to get its message out to
consumers. Promotion can be as simple as a website
ad or as complex as a trade show presentation.

Increasingly, promotion occurs online through emails, online ads, and on social media. Regardless of the form, promotional activities aim to attract customers and generate sales.

Place is where a product or service is purchased. Some products are sold directly to consumers, while others go through wholesalers or other companies before reaching the end user. Some companies sell products and services locally, while others sell across the country or internationally. The marketing team makes product placement decisions to generate the most sales.

# THE MERGING OF MARKETING AND COMPUTER SCIENCE

The marketing department is increasingly using technology and computers in their operations. More marketing efforts are moving online, via email, websites, social media, and more. In addition, digital channels, including websites, smartphones, and the internet of things (physical devices that are able to connect to the web), generate enormous amounts of data that can be captured, organized, and analyzed. Marketing automation software takes repetitive tasks and automates them, saving time and money for the company.

The rise in technology has opened the door for people who are interested in working in marketing and also have an interest in computer science and coding. Having digital skills is becoming increasingly important for success in a marketing career. Companies need

Some consumers use their smartphones to scan digital advertisements and read product reviews on websites and social media sites as they shop in physical stores.

qualified marketing professionals who can work in a digital environment. Performing a variety of roles, these people create innovative ways for marketing departments to improve their operations and provide the best information for senior executives. Armando Roggio, the director of marketing and e-commerce for a retail company, writes in an article posted on PracticalEcommerce.com:

**The ability to write code can be a huge advantage for marketers. This ability may be as basic as understanding HTML and CSS so that you can do a better job of posting articles in WordPress. Or it might be the ability to develop your own marketing tools and reports. By some estimates, half of all digital marketing jobs require at least some technical expertise. This is the case because so much of what is done online requires at least an understanding of coding.**

As marketing moves online, marketing professionals need to understand the code behind their websites and applications. "Marketers should absolutely be able to look at a website and know how that website is working and the code behind it," said Ryanair chief marketing officer (CMO) Kenny Jacobs in an interview with *Marketing Week*. "I don't believe in the model that the CMO should do the traditional marketing and the chief digital officer should do the digital marketing job. I think you should have the right customer officer doing the right job that straddles both."

In a small company, the need for marketing professionals who have coding skills is even more important. Alessandra Di Lorenzo, chief commercial officer for media and partnerships at Lastminute.com group, believes that today's marketers must become digitally literate and develop skills such as coding, website design, and data analytics. "In smaller or more integrated companies, these skills are increasingly becoming part of the marketing team's responsibility— so it's crucial teams attract the expertise to support this, and invest in training and development to plug any skills gaps that exist," she said in an interview with *Marketing Week*.

While many people in marketing careers have a degree in marketing or business, more are also developing their digital and coding skills. People working in marketing can benefit from a knowledge of software such as Adobe Creative Suite, Salesforce, and Google Analytics. Knowledge of social media, search engine optimization, and data analytics are also important to have. In addition, knowledge of programming languages such as HTML, CSS,

Many marketing professionals find that knowing how to code in various programming languages is an essential skill in today's digital marketing environment.

JavaScript, SQL, PHP, Python, Java, Ruby, and C are valuable. "Everyone should learn to code and the next generation will definitely learn how," said Dan Gilbert, CEO of marketing agency Brainlabs in an article in *Marketing Week*.

In addition to technical skills, employers are looking for people who have skills in business and project management. For many marketing careers, the ability to work well with others and communicate is critical. Many positions require a person to think creatively to design, implement, and manage effective marketing

## DIGITAL MARKETING BOOT CAMPS

Across the country, people are learning digital marketing and coding skills in specialized boot camps. Some people have a business or marketing background and want to add technical skills to make them more employable. Others are looking to switch careers and enter the marketing field for the first time.

Digital marketing boot camps are one of the fastest and most efficient ways to develop digital marketing skills. The camps run from a few weeks to several months. Some camps are part time, while other camps are full time. Students learn skills in topics such as Google Analytics, content marketing, pay-per-click advertising, marketing automation, email marketing, data science, web development, and search engine optimization. In some boot camps, students can earn certifications in various technical skills, which can give them an advantage when applying for a job.

campaigns that convince consumers to purchase products and services.

## CAREER PATHS IN MARKETING AND COMPUTER SCIENCE

People who are interested in a career that combines marketing and computer science should take classes to give them solid knowledge of marketing topics and general business skills, along with web and computer science skills. Many choose to get a business or

In technology classes at school, students might have the opportunity to ask a teacher questions about a digital marketing tool while working on collaborative projects with other students.

marketing-related degree from a four-year college, taking classes in marketing, consumer behavior, market research, business law, management, and more. Classes in computer science and programming are also beneficial. Some people choose to gain technical and programming skills by attending special coding boot camps or technology-focused graduate programs. For some positions, earning a certificate is a good way to show that a person has the technical skills needed for the career.

After earning a degree, marketing professionals work in companies of all sizes, in almost every industry. Many work for marketing or public relations companies that perform services for a portfolio of clients. Others work in a company's internal marketing department. Some marketing professionals are self-employed, working on a freelance basis for clients.

In addition to taking classes, people interested in marketing and computer science careers can take other steps to learn more about the industry. Joining a marketing professional organization can help a person learn more about the field and make contacts. Some companies offer internships to students. Internships give students the experience of working for a particular company or industry. Reading newspapers and other business and technology publications can help students keep up to date on the latest in marketing and technology.

# CHAPTER TWO

# MARKETING IN THE DIGITAL AGE

Marketing connects companies with potential customers at the right place, at the right time. Today, the internet has become a critical tool for consumers worldwide. According to a 2018 Pew Research Center survey, 77 percent of Americans go online every day. That number includes the 43 percent who say they go online several times a day and 26 percent who admit to being online almost constantly. As people spend more time on digital devices, traditional marketing through print ads or radio spots is being overtaken by email campaigns, text messages, and social media advertising. To compete, companies need to find ways to reach potential customers where they spend time—in the digital world.

# WHAT IS DIGITAL MARKETING?

Digital marketing professionals help companies promote goods and services across a number of digital channels. Digital marketing is more than creating a website or Facebook page for a company. It is using digital technology and channels to connect with potential customers and build awareness about a company and its products or services. The ultimate goal is to get a customer to make a purchase.

Digital marketing includes all online marketing efforts. Companies use online tools such as search

Your smartphone can connect you to many social media platforms such as Facebook, Instagram, Twitter, and Snapchat, as well as Google, which can be used to deliver digital marketing.

engines, social media, email, and websites to connect with customers. They design eye-catching, memorable content to get their products and services noticed by potential customers. They design digital advertising campaigns, email campaigns, and pay-per-click campaigns. They create easy-to-read online brochures. They add engaging content and interactive tools to websites and blogs. They place ads in games and mobile apps. They are active on social media channels such as Facebook, LinkedIn, Twitter, and Instagram. Each of these digital marketing activities is designed to get people to visit a company's website, buy a product or service, and come back later.

Digital marketing technologies give companies the ability to analyze marketing campaigns in real time and understand what works and what does not work. When a company places a print ad in a newspaper, it is difficult to know how many people actually read the ad vs. how many just flipped to the next page. Marketers cannot determine how many people decided to buy a product because of a specific ad. In contrast, digital marketers can use software to monitor what is being viewed on a website or social media site, how often, and for how long. Digital marketing professionals can also track what efforts turn into sales, what content engages with potential customers, and what does not. With all of this information, they can identify trends and patterns in consumers' behavior and refine marketing campaigns to achieve the best results.

For example, Domino's Pizza is using digital technology to make it easier for customers to order a pizza. Customers can order pizza via the Domino's smartphone app, on the Amazon Echo speaker, or

A group of marketing professionals collaborates on how a company's brand message is being marketing across all digital channels.

online through Facebook, Twitter, and the company website. On social media, customers can simply tweet their order to the Domino's Twitter account or use the hashtag #EasyOrder. After they order, customers can track their pizza on the app and follow its preparation and delivery status. Most of Domino's orders now come from digital platforms.

## IN THE DIGITAL MARKETING WORKPLACE

Digital marketing professionals work as part of a company's marketing team to develop online marketing strategies across websites, social media, email campaigns, mobile applications, and more. They meet with coworkers and customers to make sure that digital campaigns meet user and business needs. They work with different people and departments within a company, such as those in sales and finance. They may also work with freelance web developers, graphic designers, and other professionals.

Digital marketing professionals ensure that the company's brand message is being appropriately used across all digital channels. They develop and send email campaigns. They evaluate the look and content of websites and plan how they will be used in campaigns and advertisements. They work with the web administrators and developers to make changes and enhancements to company websites. They need to stay up to date with new and emerging digital technologies and understand current trends in digital media. They monitor, analyze, and adjust digital marketing campaigns to achieve the best outcomes. They also monitor digital channels to understand customer needs and concerns and to identify new opportunities for the company.

People working in digital marketing also use web analytics and other digital tools to gather data and information that allow them to create more effective marketing campaigns. "This person is responsible for driving relevant consumers with the goal of improving brand recognition [and] trust and ultimately drive purchase intent," said Justin Emig, a director of search marketing for Web Talent Marketing.

Adam Johnstone is the digital marketing manager at Good Energy, a renewable energy supplier based in the United Kingdom. In his role, Johnstone has set up and maintained all of the company's digital marketing channels. He has managed the development of three websites, two online customer self-serve portals, and an app. He measures the performance of digital marketing campaigns, such as email and click-through rates and various user interactions online by device, location, pages viewed, and more. To do so, he uses a variety of digital tools such as Google Analytics for data, Moz for search engine optimization, and Socialbakers for social channel management. "I love getting my hands dirty by diving in to our data to glean insight in to what is and what isn't working. This analysis allows me to improve conversion rates and ultimately user experience," he said in an interview posted on Econsultancy.com.

# WORKING TO BECOME A DIGITAL MARKETING PROFESSIONAL

Most digital marketing positions require a bachelor's degree from a four-year college or university. Some employers require a master's degree. Most people interested in this career path major in marketing, communications, digital marketing, or a related field. Regardless of one's major, courses in marketing, consumer behavior, market research, sales, and graphic design are helpful. Classes in finance, mathematics, and statistics are also good to take.

People in this career should also have strong computer and web skills. They should have experience working with digital media channels, such as websites, apps, social media, blogs, and more. They should understand digital technology platforms, content strategies, search engine optimization strategies, and user experience (UX) best practices. They should also be familiar with Google Analytics and other web measurement platforms. For many positions, having strong computer science and coding skills is valuable. Knowing programming languages such as HTML, SQL, JavaScript, and CSS make a candidate more desirable to potential employers.

Those who do not have a degree in a digital marketing field can build their skills and demonstrate proficiency by getting experience. Some students work in a digital marketing internship for a company or marketing firm. Even without a formal internship, students can build their digital skills by creating their

All accounts > www.VincentGaleano.com

**All Web Site Data** ˅

Search reports and help

HOME

CUSTOMIZATION

Reports

REAL-TIME

AUDIENCE

ACQUISITION

DISCOVER

Active Users

40 • Monthly
23

30 • Weekly
19

20 • Daily
9

Sun 06 May

| | |
|---|---|
| Monthly | 23 |
| Weekly | 19 |
| Daily | 9 |

07 Apr    14    22    29    06 May

ACTIVE USERS REPORT ＞

Last 30 days ˅

User

All Us

Mar 25

Apr 1 -

Apr 8 - A

Apr 15 -

Apr 22 - /

Apr 29 - N

Last 6 we

A digital marketing professional uses a web analytics report to analyze the effectiveness of different digital marketing efforts and create the most effective campaigns.

own blog, website, or social media channels. They can volunteer to run digital marketing campaigns for local nonprofit organizations or small businesses that need to increase their online presence.

Earning certifications are another way for candidates to demonstrate proficiency in a variety of digital skills to potential employers. "Certifications are the new degree," said Emig. Certifications such as Google AdWords, Google Analytics, Facebook Certified Planning Professional, and Hootsuite Social Marketing are in demand for many digital marketing positions.

Because the digital landscape is constantly changing, digital marketing professionals must continue to develop their marketing and computer skills and stay current on new tools and programming languages. Many keep up to date on what's happening in the industry by attending conferences and following industry blogs and websites. "Don't get complacent and never stop learning, particularly

# THE INTERNSHIP EXPERIENCE

**For three months, Sam Hull worked as a digital marketing intern for iProspect, a digital marketing company. During his internship, Hull constructed weekly and monthly campaign reports for clients. He also worked on email lead generation. He described this role in an interview on GraduateJobs.com:**

This required me getting one department to design a creative for the company. For example if BMW wanted to sell more Minis, we'd produce an email creative advertising the opportunity to test drive a Mini if you register your email address. Once you've got them signed up they are sent the link to organize the test drive and you have their details to market future ideas to them. I would then track its progress, noting sign ups, clicks, where they are clicking and compile that into a presentation to send to the client with my comments and advice.

According to Hull, the internship was a valuable experience, helping him develop his technical and business skills. It also gave him insight into digital marketing as a profession and confirmed his interest in the field.

when it comes to digital. Everything moves so fast, so it's important to stay on top of trends and not get left behind," said Johnstone.

# GROWTH IN JOB PROSPECTS

The job outlook for digital marketing is strong. According to Statista, digital marketing spending will increase from $200 billion in 2015 to $306 billion in 2020. According to the Bureau of Labor Statistics' *Occupational Outlook Handbook*, employment of advertising, promotions, and marketing managers, which includes digital marketing professionals, is projected to grow 10 percent from 2016 to 2026.

This rate of growth is faster than the average growth rate of all occupations. The main driver behind this is an increasing demand for professionals to manage digital media campaigns through websites, social media, or live chats. Candidates who can demonstrate strong digital and programming skills and have experience in SEO and social media management will have the best prospects for landing a good digital marketing job.

# CHAPTER THREE

# THE AUTOMATION OF MARKETING

M arketing activities are increasingly moving online, on websites, email, and social media. Keeping up with the volume of customers and activity across all of these digital channels is nearly impossible. According to the Global Digital Report 2018, there were more than four billion people using the internet. On social media alone, there were nearly 3.2 billion users. It takes a lot of time and money to send thousands of emails and follow-ups, post content across multiple sites, monitor and respond to social media messages, and other routine online tasks. As a result, companies are increasingly turning to marketing automation tools to help them be more productive.

## WHAT IS MARKETING AUTOMATION?

Many marketing departments are responsible for a mountain of repetitive tasks, such as sending emails to customers, posting on social media, and other

Marketing automation involves many tasks that are done together, making marketing departments more efficient.

website actions. Marketing automation takes these tasks and uses computer software and technology to automate them, which saves marketing professionals time and money. Often hosted by a third party or web-based platform, marketing automation helps marketing departments complete marketing tasks more efficiently.

In addition, marketing automation systems provide analytical tools that can make marketing departments more effective. Marketing professionals can use the automated software to send the right message to the right user at the right time. "Marketing automation is all about understanding your audience so you can adapt the way you communicate to them based on their unique buying journey," said Karra Hendrix, a product marketing manager for a marketing automation company in an article posted on CMSWire .com. "Because it allows you to track every interaction and score engagement, you can be more personalized and targeted with your messaging, while still maintaining efficiencies," said Hendrix.

For example, companies might send thousands of emails to their entire list of existing and potential customers. They hope that the message reaches some and convinces them to buy. In reality, marketers are likely wasting valuable time and money sending an email to a person who may not even be interested in the message. Even worse, some people may get annoyed at receiving multiple, impersonal emails and unsubscribe from the email list, causing the company to lose future marketing opportunities with them.

Marketing automation tools can make this process much more efficient and effective. The system creates a database of information about potential customers from tracking their actions on a website, contact form data, and other information. An automated program segments a marketer's email list and sends emails to a targeted list of potential customers, not the entire group. It can track the engagement each person has with the email—did that person click through to a website or download a brochure? Then, the program can automatically send additional information based on triggering events, such as opting in to a form or clicking through to a website.

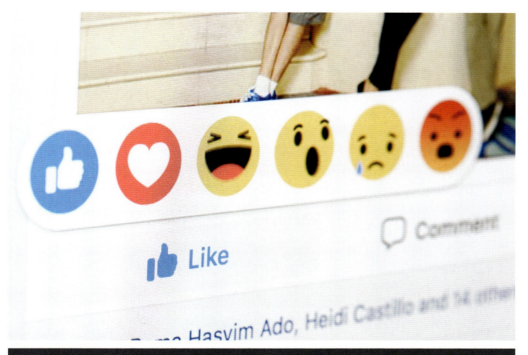

Using marketing automation software, companies can automate posting comments, "liking" posts, and engaging with customers on social media sites such as Facebook.

Once a customer opts into an email list, auto responders send out a series of emails over a set period of time. Alyssa Rimmer, director of marketing at New Breed Marketing, an inbound marketing agency, writes about this in a blog post:

This is the foundation of marketing automation. To provide you, as a marketer, with the ability to target your contacts and send them content that is based on their behavior. You're giving them the information they need when they want it. You're easing their

# WHERE O WHERE ARE THE BRIDES?

When stationary company PaperStyle wanted to improve its operations with marketing automation, it turned to Whereoware, a digital marketing agency, for help. With Whereoware's help, the company implemented a marketing automation campaign that targeted brides and their friends based on their activity in email or on PaperStyle's website.

The team began by creating a timeline of bridal buying behavior. The campaign used three triggers—clicking on a wedding link in a Paper Style email, buying wedding or bridal shower products, and visiting a wedding-related page on the PaperStyle website. If a customer hit one or more of the triggers, the automated system sent targeted emails to the customer to identify if that person was a bride or shopping for someone else.

The system then followed up with a series of wedding-themed marketing messages that advertised PaperStyle products that matched the customer's needs at the time. For example, if a bride purchased wedding favors, she would automatically receive an email promoting thank-you cards a few days later. If a bridesmaid bought a bachelorette tiara, she would receive an email customized with wedding gift ideas.

The targeted campaign was a success. The company reported that email open rates increased by 244 percent and revenue per mailing increased by 330 percent.

buying decision. And as a result, your conversion rates (and revenue) will increase.

On social media, marketing automation software allows companies to automatically distribute content across many social media platforms. Companies can also use marketing automation software to automatically engage with followers posting comments and likes based on specific criteria. Marketers can also use automation programs to send confirmation, reminder, and thank-you emails, promote upcoming events, send new product promotions, and follow up with customers who abandon their online shopping cart before completing a purchase. Rimmer said of this process:

> Marketing automation has helped me streamline my own process and gives me greater visibility into what my visitors and leads are actually doing. I can quickly find what content they're downloading, how they are responding to my emails, and how they are moving through the sales funnel.

## WORKING IN MARKETING AUTOMATION

People in this career implement automated marketing systems to grow and support a company's overall marketing strategies. They need to have a good understanding of business and marketing work processes, or workflows, so that they can design automated processes to achieve company goals. They are also responsible for getting different technologies and systems to work together efficiently. They manage marketing automation systems, develop automated email strategies to increase customer engagement and growth, and use software tools to create automated landing pages, which are stand-alone web pages created specifically for a marketing campaign.

People who are interested in working in marketing automation careers may begin in email marketing, where they use the HTML computer language to build email marketing campaigns. As they gain experience, they can take on more responsibilities. The marketing automation team will work with managers and other

A digital professional works on code for a program that will automate a new advertising email campaign for the marketing department.

team members to review data sets and make sure the marketing automation system is capturing meaningful information for marketing executives. They set up marketing automation and customer relationship management (CRM) platforms to work together and produce synchronized reports. Some marketing automation professionals advance to become managers or marketing executives within a company.

Jeana Abboud is a marketing automation specialist for Social Factor, a marketing agency. In her role, she works with clients to plan, build, and execute marketing automation tools. She spends a lot of time researching trends in email marketing and automation. Abboud believes that staying current on the latest technology in the field is an important part of her job. "Whether it's HubSpot, MailChimp or other email and automation tools, learning to build, test and manage campaigns with various clients is important. Since every tool has different capabilities, it's important to stay ahead of the game in lead nurturing campaigns, email blasts, reporting and more," she said in an interview posted on SocialFactor.com.

## GETTING ON TRACK FOR A JOB IN MARKETING AUTOMATION

Most people who work in marketing automation have at least a bachelor's degree in business, marketing, computer science, or a related field from a four-year college or university. Some employers prefer someone with a master's degree. Computer and technology skills

Marketo (www.marketo.com) is one type of marketing automation software that helps professionals engage potential and existing customers efficiently and effectively.

are also important for this career. Students should take classes and develop skills in the computer languages SQL, HTML, CSS, JavaScript, and Python.

Many employers also want candidates to have experience using marketing automation platforms such as Marketo, ExactTarget, Eloqua, Pardot, and Salesforce Marketing. Many students complete an internship at a marketing firm or department to gain hands-on experience in marketing automation. Earning certifications is another way to demonstrate proficiency in marketing and technical skills to potential employers.

In addition to having strong computer skills, people working in marketing automation careers should be creative, have good analytical skills, and be detail oriented. These skills help them evaluate how marketing automation can help a company meet business and sales objectives. People in this career should also have excellent communication and interpersonal skills. They often work closely as members of a team and present information to company executives. When dealing with a wide variety of people, they must be able to explain technical topics in an easy-to-understand way.

## THE JOB OUTLOOK

The job outlook for digital marketing, including marketing automation, is strong. According to the Bureau of Labor Statistics' *Occupational Outlook Handbook*, employment of advertising, promotions, and marketing managers, which includes marketing automation professionals, is projected to grow 10 percent from 2016 to 2026.

As digital campaigns increase, the demand for professionals who can manage marketing automation software and strategies will also grow. Candidates who can demonstrate strong digital and programming skills and have experience working with marketing automation software will have the best prospects for landing a good job in marketing automation.

# CHAPTER FOUR

# MARKETING AND WEB DEVELOPMENT

With the growth of the internet, all businesses require state-of-the-art websites. Having a website is an important way to get a company's marketing in front of customers. Potential customers visit an organization's website to research the business, learn more about its products, find store locations, and read customer reviews. In turn, companies and organizations use their websites to advertise services, publicize activities, and raise awareness about certain causes, missions, or endeavors.

Increasingly, consumers are making purchases online. "Purchases online have continued to grow—double-digit growth year in, year out—for the last 10 years," said Steve Tissenbaum, a professor at Toronto's Ted Rogers School of Management in an article posted on Workopolis.com. "And it's not going

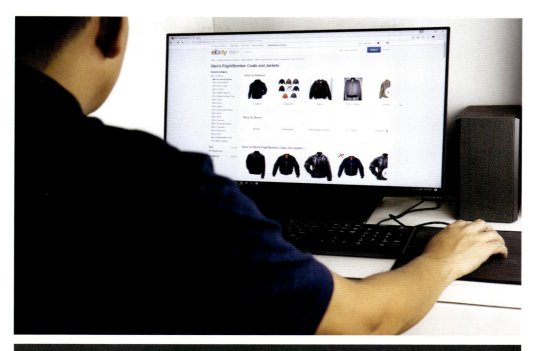

A highly effective and professional website, such as that of Ebay (www.ebay.com), is an essential part of a business's marketing platform.

This boom in online sales makes it essential that companies have well-designed and user-friendly websites. Some of the best websites incorporate technical features such as e-commerce software, graphics, videos, and other applications. While a great website can be an invaluable marketing tool, not having a website can cause a company to miss out on sales. If potential customers cannot find a company online, they simply move on to the next company that has an easy-to-find and easy-to-use website.

# WHAT GOES INTO CREATING A GREAT WEBSITE?

Website developers create the layout, color scheme, and general design of websites. They create specialized, eye-catching sites for many industries. They are also responsible for a site's technical aspects, including its performance (speed) and capacity (traffic). They may work for a company or organization directly or be hired independently. Because every organization is different, web developers work with each client to create an individual design. They consider a client's products and services when designing the site. After the site is built, they regularly adjust and add updates to it. In some cases, web developers also create content for the site.

For e-commerce, developers must consider the needs of both online customers and companies. Companies must make sure their websites are easy to access from all devices, including computers, tablets, and smartphones. Photos, videos, and other multimedia content must load quickly or customers will lose patience and leave the site. Customers must also be able to easily navigate the site and products so that they can quickly search and purchase items from different devices. Behind the scenes, the site must be easy to update and add new products, information, and images. Often, companies will also want their e-commerce sites to integrate smoothly with back-office software, such as accounting systems,

E-commerce technology allows you to shop online using a tablet computer and use a credit card to make a purchase without leaving your home.

customer relationship management software, and inventory and shipping systems.

# LIFE AS A WEB DEVELOPER

Web developers design and create websites. They are responsible for the site's appearance and its technical features. These include the site's performance or speed and its capacity, which is the amount of user traffic it can handle. Some web developers also create content for sites.

# CAREER PROFILE: CHRIS SEAN

After bouncing around in a few different jobs, Chris Sean decided to take his career in a new direction. He spent three months taking classes and learning how to code and develop websites.

After a lot of hard work, Sean landed a job as a junior front-end developer with a company. Within a year, he was promoted to become the company's main front-end developer. Since then, Sean has worked developing websites and e-commerce sites for a variety of clients.

In an interview posted on technology school Treehouse's website, Sean talked about his job as a web developer:

I wear many hats at work. I work on anything from regular donation/payment pages for our business merchants to crazy customized e-commerce pages for our bigger clients. I've worked with big clients from universities to well-known non-profit organizations. Believe it or not, I've even worked on a registration page for Kevin Durant's Foundation! Since then, I've started a YouTube Channel to help encourage other aspiring developers like myself to take that first leap in code as I share my life as a web developer. I've had the chance to see people of all ages from around the world get hired as developers since I started my channel. Nothing beats knowing that I've helped change the lives of many people around the world.

In a typical day, a web developer might meet with clients or coworkers to talk about the function and design of a website. Web developers write code for websites, often using programming languages such as HTML, CSS, and JavaScript. They create and test applications for the site. They work with other team members and designers to determine a site's information, function, and layout. They incorporate graphics, audio, and video into the site. Once the site is up and running, web developers monitor traffic, make adjustments or additions as necessary, and troubleshoot any problems.

While some web developers handle every part of a website's construction from design to maintenance, others specialize in certain areas. Back-end web developers focus on how a site operates. They oversee the website's technical construction. They create the site's basic framework and make sure that it works as designed. Back-end developers also determine the process for adding new pages and information to the website. In contrast, front-end web developers focus more on how a site looks and how users interact with it. They create layouts and integrate graphics, applications, and other content. Front-end developers often write web programs in computer languages such as HTML or JavaScript. Once a website is up and running, webmasters maintain and update them.

Bethanne Zink is a web developer who works for Bounce Exchange, an online marketing analytics company. She spends about 60 percent of her time building features on clients' websites, while the rest of her time is split between answering questions and troubleshooting website issues. When working to add features to a client's existing website, "I extensively familiarize myself with the client's website, so as to write code that jives perfectly with their existing code," said Zink in an interview posted on Skillcrush.com. "Today, I'm writing code that hooks into the API for the email service provider of one of our e-commerce clients. It's a project that I've tackled for many of our other clients, but is always a little bit different, and entails playing with API calls, which is my favorite thing to do." Zink says that one of the biggest challenges of her job is writing code that works across different web

A marketing professional reviews a data analytics report to get metrics on a company's website and its web traffic.

browsers and devices and integrates with the clients' sites. "We work on a lot of different sites and every one is a different snowflake, which poses a challenge, but also keeps things interesting," said Zink. "It's fun to dive into clients' sites and see how other developers are building and designing their little piece of the Web."

# WORKING TOWARD A CAREER IN WEB DEVELOPMENT

Most web developers have at least an associate's degree in web design or a related field. For more technical jobs, some employers want employees to have at least a bachelor's degree in computer science, programming, or a related field. Taking courses in graphic design can also be helpful, especially if the web developer will be involved in creating a website's visual appearance.

Web developers should have strong technical and web programming skills. They must be proficient in HTML, the markup language for making web pages. Developers should also have strong technical skills in other programming languages, such as JavaScript and CSS, and be able to work with multimedia publishing tools such as Flash. Back-end developers, who focus on the functionality behind a great-looking website, should have a good working knowledge of programming languages such as PHP, Python, Java, and MySQL. Because the computer science environment is always changing, web developers must continue to

A web programmer will work for hours to write and review code to create a new website for a company that will include several features, including an online store.

develop new computer skills and stay current on new tools and programming languages.

In addition to strong technical skills, web developers should also have several other qualities and skills to be successful. Because web developers often spend a lot of time at a computer, writing detailed code for hours, the ability to concentrate and focus on small details is extremely important. A tiny error in the HTML code could cause an entire webpage to stop working. Successful web developers are often very creative people, which can help them design a website's appearance and make sure it is innovative and fresh. Web developers should also have excellent communication and interpersonal skills to communicate effectively with coworkers, management, and clients.

# THE JOB OUTLOOK

The job outlook for web developers is very good. According to the Bureau of Labor Statistics' *Occupational Outlook Handbook*, employment of web developers is projected to grow 15 percent from 2016 to 2026. This rate of growth is much faster than the average of all occupations. This growth is being driven by the increase in e-commerce. As more people buy goods and services online, the need for web developers to create and maintain e-commerce websites will grow.

In addition, the growing use of mobile devices will also increase the number of opportunities, as developers will be needed to create sites that work on mobile devices and multiple screen sizes. Candidates who have strong technical skills and knowledge of multiple programming languages and digital multimedia tools will have the best opportunities for working as a web developer.

# THE WORLD OF MARKETING ANALYTICS

Data analytics is the process of examining raw data to draw conclusions about it. Using powerful computers and analytics programs, businesses can identify patterns and relationships in data and use that information to help them make immediate decisions. This leads to more sales, reduced costs, more efficient operations, and more satisfied employees and customers.

In marketing, data comes from marketing campaigns, sales, websites, customer surveys, social media, financial records, operations, and more. To make sense of all this data, marketing departments use analytics to help them evaluate, analyze, and manage marketing activities. Using marketing analytics, companies can identify which specific marketing efforts are successful, which need improvement, and how they can be improved. The goal of analytics is to help managers to make marketing and business decisions that increase company profits

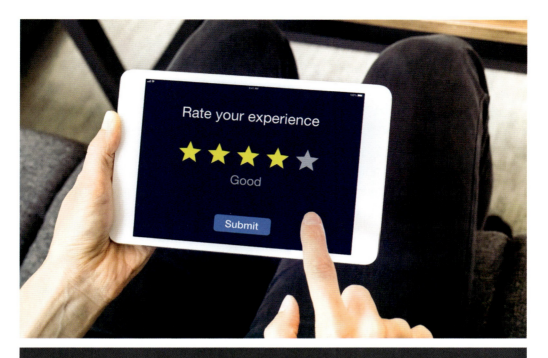

A customer uses a tablet computer to post a customer satisfaction rating on a company website and gives the product or service a four out of five stars.

One way companies are using marketing analytics is to improve the customer experience. With data from sales, social media, websites, surveys, and more, marketing analytics provides insight on customers' likes and dislikes and how likely they are to engage with a company's products or services. Using this information, companies can better provide the products and services that meet customer needs and wants.

Delivering a great customer experience and consistently providing what customers want, and when they want it, can help a company stand out in a crowded marketplace. "The most successful companies use analytics to understand how well they generate demand and the quality of the customer experience they provide," says Joerg Niessing, a marketing professor at the graduate business school INSEAD in an article in *Harvard Business Review*. "If you want to have a major impact, you need an integrated approach to see what is happening at all customer touch points and understand how effective you are."

Once a company collects and analyzes customer data, marketing analytics can help identify patterns of customer behavior that suggest ways to create a better customer experience. For example, at Progressive Insurance, the marketing group wanted to improve customer satisfaction with their mobile app. They collected data on how users of the mobile app were behaving. Looking at this data, they discovered that users wanted more than helpful insurance quotes in the app; they also wanted to purchase insurance via the app. In response, Progressive gave them what they wanted, the ability to buy insurance via the company's app, which improved the overall customer experience and increased sales.

## WORKING IN MARKETING ANALYTICS

Companies in every industry need data analysts to make sense of all the data they receive and put it into a useful and understandable format. Data analysts use their skills in math, statistics, and computer science to gather and organize enormous amounts of data. Then they use analytical skills and industry and marketing knowledge to reach meaningful conclusions. A data analyst writes algorithms to analyze large amounts of data. He or she builds predictive models and software to help a company make decisions.

Each day, a data analyst may perform a variety of tasks. He or she develops systems to collect huge volumes of data from a variety of sources. A data analyst operates sophisticated analytics programs and

Progressive Insurance improved its app to allow customers to purchase insurance directly through their smartphones.

statistical methods to prepare data for analysis. He or she uses software programs to cleanse data, or eliminate irrelevant information from it. A data analyst examines the data from different perspectives to identify trends, opportunities, and weaknesses. He or she creates algorithms to solve problems and builds tools to automate work. He or she also prepares reports that communicate findings and results for management.

"As an analyst, I spend a significant amount of time producing and maintaining both internal and client-facing reports," said marketing analyst Casey Pearson in an article posted on the Rasmussen College website. Writing up a report is much more than summarizing numbers on a page: data analysts spot patterns and trends and communicate them to others. "To remain valuable, the reports, answers and insights data analysis provides have to be understood by the next decision-maker, who frequently is not an analyst," says manager of analytics Jess Kendra in the Rasmussen College website article.

People who enjoy working with numbers and data might be a good fit for a career in marketing analytics. They may start as data analysts or marketing specialists and advance to roles as analytics managers and marketing executives. Most people working in this career have at least a bachelor's degree from a four-year college or university, although some candidates earn a master's degree.

People interested in pursuing this career often major in subjects such as marketing analytics, statistics, or data science. Taking courses in math and statistics prepares students to work in data analyst jobs. These courses can help students develop the technical skills they will need in linear algebra, calculus, probability, statistical hypothesis testing, and summary statistics. In addition, students should take courses to develop business, marketing, and research skills. Earning marketing analytics certifications can also demonstrate a student's skill and commitment to the field.

Computer science skills are critical for data analysts. Analysts must be able to work with analytical tools and software such as Excel, R, SAS, and STATA. Having some coding skills, especially in programming languages such as Python, C/C++, Java, and Perl, is valuable. In addition, data analysts should be skilled in working with SQL databases and database querying languages. They should also be comfortable using tools such as Google Analytics, Visual Website Optimizer, Google Tag Manager, Tableau, and Google AdWords. Because the computer science environment is always changing, people working in marketing analytics must continue to develop new computer skills and stay current on new tools and programming languages.

In addition to strong technical skills, several skills are important for people working in marketing analytics. Problem-solving strategies are also important because data analysts have to create new ways of looking at and analyzing data. Data analysts should have excellent communication and interpersonal skills as many work closely with others in a team. In addition, data analysts must be able to communicate effectively with management and others who may not have a technical background.

As the field of marketing analytics is constantly changing, candidates must stay up to date on the latest trends. They can do this by taking an

A team of data analysts studies marketing analytics as they decide what information will be most useful to include in a report for marketing and company executives.

online marketing analytics class, attending industry conferences, and reading marketing analytics blogs.

## LOOKING TO THE FUTURE

As marketing analytics becomes essential for company success, the job outlook for marketing data analysts is very good. According to the Bureau of Labor Statistics' *Occupational Outlook Handbook*, employment of market research analysts and

## CAREER PROFILE: CHRIS DOWSETT, MARKETING ANALYTICS

Chris Dowsett is the head of marketing analytics at photo and video social media platform Instagram. He believes that marketing analytics is the foundation of any successful marketing program. According to Dowsett, working in marketing analytics is much more than website clicks and converting clicks to sales. It's an often-unpredictable mix of dashboards, algorithms, coding, and consulting.

This variety from week to week is what drew Dowsett to the career. Dowsett wrote in an article posted on the Towards Data Science website:

> The reason I love my job is that my day can vary from light SQL coding through to full-blown machine-learning algorithms. My role is diverse and has impact; my analyses drive multi-million dollar decisions. I have the opportunity to meet with everyone from the CFO to energetic interns. And I look at data across the ecosystem. I review data on every product area and deep-dive into the relationship between product behavior, demographic information and cultural trends.

marketing specialists, which includes marketing analytics, is projected to grow 23 percent from 2016 to 2026. This rate of growth is much faster than the average of all occupations. This growth is driven by the increasing use of data and marketing research across all companies.

Marketing analytics professionals will be needed to collect and analyze data from a number of sources to help understand the needs and wants of customers, measure the effectiveness of marketing campaigns and business strategies, and identify the factors that affect customer experience and product demand. With this information, companies can design marketing strategies to be more effective and efficient.

Since more companies are realizing the value of marketing analytics, the job prospects for this career field are good. Candidates who have a master's degree in marketing, statistics, marketing analytics, or a related field, as well as a strong background in statistics and data analysis will have the best prospects for landing a good job in marketing analytics.

# CHAPTER SIX

# THE ABCS OF SEO

Today, there are more than one billion websites on the internet. Imagine a person who wants to research and buy new hockey skates online. They type "best hockey skates" into a search engine such as Google, Yahoo, or Bing. The search engine returns a list of websites that have something to do with hockey skates and which ones are the best—blogs, reviews, stores, and manufacturers. The user clicks on one of the links near the top of the list, rather than scrolling through the list and clicking on one further down. For the first company, being listed higher is a definite advantage. How does a website get listed higher on the search engine's results? The answer is search engine optimization, or SEO.

## WHAT IS SEARCH ENGINE OPTIMIZATION?

Search engines help users find information and websites on the internet. When a user enters a specific query into the search engine, the engine

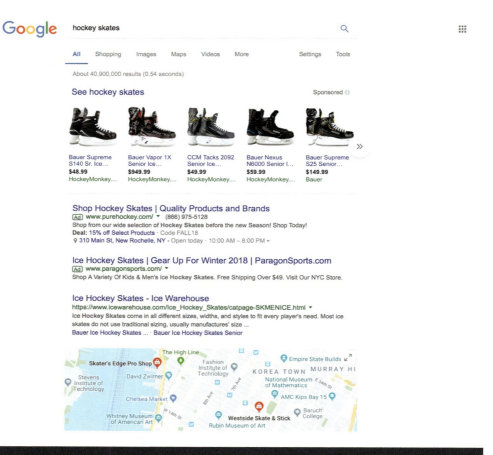

Marketing professionals work to ensure that when a user enters certain keywords into Google (www.google.com) or a similar search engine, their website is listed high on the first page.

returns a list of search results that match the query's keywords. To do this, search engines use web robots and spiders to crawl the web, moving site to site and page to page. An algorithm creates an index from the pages the engine reads. Another algorithm receives the user's search query, matches it to information in the index, and returns the search results.

Every search engine uses its own algorithm to rank webpages to make sure only relevant results are returned to a user's query. That's why different search engines might return different results. For example, Google and Bing will probably give different results for the same search query because each uses certain factors to rank website pages. Some of these factors include content, keywords, tags, and more.

Search engine optimization is the process of optimizing a website so that search engines show it as one of the top results for searches that include specific keywords. SEO incorporates technical work, which includes how quickly a page loads to how it is coded, it also includes a site's content, making sure the webpage best answers users' questions. In addition, SEO includes how much online buzz is generated about a site or page, usually measured by how many others have shared or linked to the page.

Why is it so important to be in a search engine's top results? According to a study by Advanced Web Ranking, the first five results on a Google search get nearly 68 percent of clicks, which indicates users clicking through to the website. Results that rank sixth to tenth get only 4 percent. And if a website is listed on the second page of search results, few users will click through to visit it.

SEO has become important in marketing because it helps companies make their websites and businesses more visible to online users. In 2015, Barrington All Makes, an auto repair company, began working with a digital marketing firm to improve their website. They wanted to increase their

Following the steps in the search engine optimization process can help a company improve its website's search ranking so that it is seen by more potential customers.

online presence and attract more customers. "Our business didn't come up in search engines and our web site was very outdated and needed to be brought into this century," said Barrington's Karen Noury in a case study posted on the Make It Active website. The digital marketing firm created a new dynamic website for the auto repair company that incorporated SEO strategies. The new website and SEO work were a success. Barrington reported a

1,400 percent increase in traffic to its website and a 32 percent increase in revenue.

To help them appear higher in search engine results, companies are turning to specialized marketing professionals called SEO specialists. SEO specialists design, develop, and promote high-quality websites. They make sure a company's website incorporates the latest SEO standards. They evaluate keywords, backlinks, formatting, and content to redesign and create the optimal website. In addition, they generate content—text, graphics, or other types— that help raise a website's ranking. "Ultimately we convince search engines that we provide the best answer to a question someone might ask," said Tony Tie, a senior SEO specialist for travel website Expedia, in an article on the *Globe and Mail* website. "If you're number one, if you're higher up on [the results page], people are more likely to click on you, which leads to more transactions." While some SEO specialists work directly for a company, others work as freelancers or for a consulting firm.

Some SEO professionals specialize in specific parts of SEO. Some become content writers and produce short articles and other content necessary to raise a site's search engine results pages. Some specialize in link building. As more search engines use backlinking—the practice of another page linking to a company's website—in their search algorithms, developing backlinks to the company's website from reliable websites is important. Some SEO specialists focus on web research and provide valuable information about the latest SEO guidelines and background information for content writers, web developers, and link builders.

## WHAT IT TAKES TO BECOME AN SEO SPECIALIST

Many employers require SEO specialists to have a bachelor's degree from a four-year college or university,

### CAREER PROFILE: JACK SAVILLE, SEO SPECIALIST

Jack Saville is an SEO specialist for Bynder, a digital-asset management provider in Amsterdam. One of his job duties is to monitor the website's performance daily and identify any significant fluctuations in traffic. He creates and edits content on the site to incorporate specific keywords that will help it rise in search engine rankings. He also tests the site regularly to identify and fix any issues that arise that could impact its rankings. "My favourite thing about working in SEO is the satisfaction of seeing how the changes you have made have helped to significantly improve search rankings," he said in an article posted on econsultancy.com. "As I think a lot of SEOs will agree, it can sometimes be frustrating if people don't follow your recommendations. But this can be easily fixed with a quick chat to explain the potential benefit they are missing out on."

although some positions accept an associate's degree. People interested in SEO careers often major in information technology, business, marketing, communications, or a related field. They should also take classes in web design, web content production, and programming languages such as HTML and CSS.

Strong technical skills are a must for a career in SEO. SEO professionals need to be able to program in HTML or PHP, use database management software like MySQL and data mining software such as Google Analytics, and use marketing software such as AdWords or Marketo Marketing Automation. Jack Saville, SEO specialist, said in an article on econsultancy.com:

> **Technical skills are also very important, as they allow me to identify technical obstacles to our search engine ranking improvement. For example, having knowledge of HTML, CSS and JSON-LD means that I know what I need to do to make sure that our site is technically optimized for search engines.**

In addition, SEO professionals should have strong analytical skills to be able to analyze client websites and determine the effectiveness of marketing strategies. Communication skills are also needed as they often work as part of a team.

Because the SEO industry changes so rapidly, experience and ongoing education are essential for success in this career. SEO professionals must keep their skill sets up to date and learn the latest

Stephen Allan, CEO of MediaCom (*left*), gestures as he speaks onstage with Tim Armstrong, CEO of AOL Inc., at a digital marketing conference.

search engine criteria. As search engines like Google and Yahoo update their search algorithms, SEO specialists must know about these changes on a timely basis and be able to update their clients' websites to raise their rankings. To stay current on the latest industry developments, SEO professionals attend conferences and workshops where they can talk with industry experts and peers. They learn valuable information from SEO webinars and training videos. They also read blogs written by SEO experts. Some specialists choose to earn SEO certifications to show they have mastered the skills necessary for the career.

# THE FUTURE FOR SEO SPECIALISTS

The job outlook for SEO specialists is good. According to the Bureau of Labor Statistics' *Occupational Outlook Handbook*, employment of market research analysts and marketing specialists, which includes SEO specialists, is projected to grow 23 percent from 2016 to 2026. As more people rely on the internet to research products and make purchasing decisions, companies will need to employ professionals with the right skills to make sure their websites are being seen by as many people as possible.

"SEO experts are definitely in demand. There are more and more businesses that understand that launching a website is just the beginning of building their online presence," said Inessa Bokhan, cofounder and chief internet marketing manager at a startup SEO agency, in an article posted on the Link-Assistant.com blog. In addition, professionals with strong SEO skills and experience can often move into other digital and content marketing jobs. Candidates who have strong technical skills and knowledge of search engine criteria, web design and content production, and multiple programming languages and digital multimedia tools will have the best opportunities for having successful careers in SEO.

# GLOSSARY

**algorithm**  A process or set of rules to be followed in calculations, often by a computer.

**automation**  The use of technology to perform a task without human intervention.

**backlink**  The practice of another web page linking to a company's website.

**certification**  An official document that shows a level of achievement.

**data analytics**  The science of examining raw data and drawing conclusions from the information.

**database**  A set of data held in a computer.

**e-commerce**  Commercial transactions that take place over the internet.

**engagement**  Online interaction measured through clicks, likes, posts, or other activity.

**freelance**  A term used to describe a worker who is self-employed.

**index**  A list of words or phrases created by search engines that point to related websites and pages.

**integrate**  To combine one thing with another so that they work together as a whole.

**internship**  The position of a student or trainee who works in an organization, sometimes without pay, in order to gain work experience.

**keyword**  The words and phrases users enter into search engines.

**mobile app**  A computer program designed to run on a mobile device, such as a phone, tablet or watch.

**multimedia**  Content that uses several different forms, such as text, audio, images, animations, and video.

**optimize**  To rearrange or rewrite data or software to improve the efficiency of retrieval or processing.

**processor**  A part of a computer that performs calculations and manipulates data.

**profits**  The difference between the amount earned and the amount spent, usually relating to a business.

**promotion**  Activities aimed at increasing awareness, creating interest, generating sales, or creating brand loyalty.

**American Marketing Association (AMA)**
130 E. Randolph Street, 22nd Floor,
Chicago, IL 60601
(800) AMA-1150
Website: http://www.ama.org
Facebook: @AmericanMarketing
Twitter: @AMA_Marketing
The AMA is a professional organization for marketing
   professionals. It hosts conferences, trainings,
   and virtual events for marketers, researchers, and
   students in all stages of their careers.

**Association of Information Technology Professionals
   (AITP)**
1120 Route 73, Suite 200
Mount Laurel, NJ 08054-5113
(800) 224-9371
Website: http://www.aitp.org
Twitter: @CompTIAAITP
AITP works to advance the information technology
   profession through professional development,
   education, and national policies. It features
   webinars, conferences, awards for professionals
   and students, a career center with a jobs board,
   and networking options that are of interest to
   computer science professionals.

**Association of Software Professionals (ASP)**
PO Box 1522
Martinsville, IN 46151
(765) 349-4740

Website: http://asp-software.org
Facebook: @AssocSoftwareProfessionals
The ASP is a professional trade association of
    software developers and provides a community
    for software developers to share information
    about the industry.

**Canada's Association of Information Technology**
    **Professionals (CIPS)**
60 Bristol Road East
Unit 8, Suite #324
Mississauga, Ontario
L4Z 3K8
Canada
(905) 602-1370
Website: http://www.cips.ca
Facebook: @CIPS.ca
Twitter: @CIPS
CIPS represents thousands of professionals in the
    Canadian IT industry and provides networking
    opportunities, certification of IT professionals,
    accreditation of university and college programs,
    and an IT job board. The organization also advocates
    to the Canadian government on issues that affect the
    IT industry and professionals in Canada.

**CompTIA**
3500 Lacey Road, Suite 100
Downers Grove, IL 60515
(630) 678-8300
Website: https://www.comptia.org
Facebook and Twitter: @CompTIA

CompTIA provides many IT certifications and education resources for professionals in information technology. The organization also advocates for the IT industry at the local, state, and federal government levels.

**IEEE Computer Society**
3 Park Avenue, 17th Floor
New York, NY 10016
Website: http://www.ieee.org
Facebook: @ieeecomputersociety
Twitter: @ComputerSociety
The IEEE Computer Society is the world's largest professional organization for advancing technology and engineering globally. It provides many publications, conferences, technology standards, and professional and educational activities that those interested in software development will find useful.

**Information Technology Association of Canada**
5090 Explorer Drive, Suite 510
Mississauga, Ontario
L4W 4T9
Canada
(905) 602-8345
Website: http://itac.ca
Twitter: @ITAC_Online
The Information Technology Association of Canada supports the development of a digital economy in Canada. It represents information technology professionals in a wide variety of industries.

International Web Association (IWA)
556 S. Fair Oaks Avenue, #101-200
Pasadena, CA 91105
Website: http://iwanet.org
The IWA is the industry's recognized leader in providing
educational and certification standards for web
professionals. The association supports more
than three hundred thousand individual members
in 106 countries.

**National Association of Programmers**
PO Box 529
Prairieville, LA 70769
Website: http://www.napusa.org
The association is for programmers, developers,
consultants, and other professionals and students
in the computer industry. It provides information
and resources for members, including articles,
certification, events, and more.

# FOR FURTHER READING

Bedell, J. M. *So, You Want to Be a Coder? The Ultimate Guide to a Career in Programming, Video Game Creation, Robotics, and More!* New York, NY: Aladdin, 2016.

Berger, Jonah. *Contagious: Why Things Catch On*. New York, NY: Simon & Schuster, 2016.

Godin, Seth. *This Is Marketing*. New York, NY: Portfolio/Penguin, 2018.

Harmon, Daniel. *Careers as a Marketing and Public Relations Specialist*. New York, NY: Rosen Publishing, 2014.

Holiday, Ryan. *Growth Hacker Marketing: A Primer on the Future of PR, Marketing, and Advertising*. New York, NY: Portfolio/Penguin, 2014.

Kassnoff, David. *What Degree Do I Need to Pursue a Career in Information Technology & Information Systems?* New York, NY: Rosen Publishing, 2014.

La Bella, Laura. *Becoming a Data Engineer*. New York, NY: Rosen Young Adult, 2017.

La Bella, Laura. *Building Apps*. New York, NY: Rosen Publishing, 2015.

Lowe, Doug. *Java All-in-One For Dummies*. Hoboken, NJ: John Wiley & Sons, 2014.

Macarthy, Andrew. *500 Social Media Marketing Tips: Essential Advice, Hints and Strategy for Business: Facebook, Twitter, Pinterest, YouTube, Instagram, Snapchat, LinkedIn, and More!* North Charleston, SC: CreateSpace, 2018.

Matthes, Eric. *Python Crash Course: A Hands-On, Project-Based Introduction to Programming*. San Francisco, CA: No Starch Press, 2015.

Nieuwland, Jackson. *Careers for Tech Girls in E-Commerce*. New York, NY: Rosen Publishing, 2018.

Niver, Heather. *Careers for Tech Girls in Computer Science*. New York, NY: Rosen Publishing, 2014.

Payment, Simone. *Getting to Know Python! Code Power: A Teen Programmer's Guide*. New York, NY: Rosen Publishing, 2014.

Scott, David Meerman. *The New Rules of Marketing & PR: How to Use Social Media, Online Video, Mobile Applications, Blogs, News Releases, and Viral Marketing to Reach Buyers Directly*. Hoboken, NJ: John Wiley & Sons, 2017.

# BIBLIOGRAPHY

Abboud, Jeana. "A Day in the Life: Marketing Automation Specialist." Social Factor.com. Retrieved October 1, 2018. https://socialfactor .com/day-life-marketing-automation-specialist.

Allocadia. "A Day in the Life of a World-Class MarketingOps Pro: An Interview with Commvault's Anna Soo." Retrieved October 1, 2018. https:// content.allocadia.com/blog/a-day-in-the-life-of-a -world-class-marketing-ops-pro.

Davis, Ben. "A Day in the Life of…a Client-Side SEO Specialist." Econsultancy.com, March 14, 2017. https://econsultancy .com/a-day-in-the-life-of-a-client-side-seo-specialist.

Gabdulkhakova, Olga. "Is SEO a Good Career Choice? 14 Top Experts Know the Answer." Link-Assistant .com. Retrieved October 1, 2018. https://www.link -assistant.com/blog/seo-career.

Gilliland, Nikki. "A Day in the Life of…Digital Marketing Manager for Good Energy." Econsultancy.com, April 27, 2017. https://econsultancy.com/blog/69045 -a-day-in-the-life-of-digital-marketing-manager-for -good-energy.

GraduateJobs.com. "My Internship Experience in… Digital Marketing with Sam Hull." Retrieved October 1, 2018. https://www.graduate-jobs.com/internships /digital-marketing-internship-case-study.jsp.

*Harvard Business Review*. "Marketing Analytics Can Improve the Customer Experience." August 9, 2016. https://hbr.org/sponsored/2016/08/marketing -analytics-can-improve-the-customer-experience.

Make it Active. "SEO Case Study." Retrieved October 1, 2018. https://www.makeitactive.com /case-studies/small-business-seo-case-study.

Malvik, Callie. "What Does a Data Analyst Do? Exploring the Day-to-Day of This Tech Career." Rasmussen College, May 21, 2018. http://www .rasmussen.edu/degrees/technology/blog /what-does-a-data-analyst-do.

Morgan, Jackie. "A Day in the Life of a Junior Developer." Skillcrush.com, May 7, 2018. https:// skillcrush.com/2016/06/09 /junior-developer-daily-life.

Nicastro, Dom. "What Is Marketing Automation and How Does It Help Marketers?" CMSWire .com, February 8, 2018. http://www.cmswire .com/marketing-automation/what-is-marketing -automation-and-how-does-it-help-marketers.

Paliwal, Kavita. "Coding for Marketers." LoginRadius .com. Retrieved October 1, 2018. https://www .loginradius.com/fuel/coding-for-marketers.

Peltz, James F. "Domino's Pizza Stock Is Up 5,000% Since 2008. Here's Why." *Los Angeles Times*, May 15, 2017. http://www.latimes.com/business/la-fi -agenda-dominos-20170515-story.html.

Rimmer, Alyssa. "What Is Marketing Automation? A Beginner's Guide." HubSpot.com. Retrieved October 1, 2018. https://blog.hubspot.com.

Rogers, Charlotte. "The Big Debate: Is Coding a Must-Have Skill for Marketers?" *Marketing Week*, May 15, 2017. https://www.marketingweek .com/2017/05/15 /the-big-debate-marketers-coding.

Roggio, Armando. "9 Ecommerce Marketing Skills That Drive Success." PracticalEcommerce.com, April 20, 2016. https://www.practicalecommerce.com /9-Ecommerce-Marketing-Skills-that-Drive-Success.

Talley, Jenell. "What Does a Digital Marketing Manager Do?" MediaBistro.com. Retrieved October 1, 2018. https://www.mediabistro.com/climb-the -ladder/skills-expertise/what-does-a-digital -marketing-manager-do.

Workopolis.com. "Why E-Comm Careers Are a Hot Commodity." November 27, 2017. https://careers .workopolis.com/advice/careers-e-commerce -hot-commodity.

# INDEX

# ABOUT THE AUTHOR

Carla Mooney is a graduate of the University of Pennsylvania. Before becoming an author, she spent several years working in finance as an accountant. Today, she writes for young people and is the author of many books for young adults and children. Mooney enjoys learning about new technologies and the impact they will have on different industries and the average consumer.

# PHOTO CREDITS

Cover andresr/E+/Getty Images; back cover, pp. 4–5 (background) nadla/E+/Getty Images; p. 5 (inset) Rocketclips, Inc./Shutterstock.com; pp. 8, 18, 28, 38, 48, 57 (background) jijomathaidesigners/Shutterstock.com, (circuit pattern) Titima Ongkantong/Shutterstock.com; p. 9 Vladimir Mucibabic/Shutterstock.com; p. 12 antoniodiaz/Shutterstock.com; p. 14 Best-Backgrounds /Shutterstock.com; p. 16 goodluz/Shutterstock.com; p. 19 BigTunaOnline/Shutterstock.com; p. 21 Dima Sidelnikov/Shutterstock.com; p. 25 GaleanoStock /Shutterstock.com; p. 29 stoatphoto/Shutterstock.com; p. 31 PixieMe/Shutterstock.com; p. 34 Arturs Budkevics /Shutterstock.com; p. 36 Jarretera/Shutterstock.com; p. 39 Jasni/Shutterstock.com; p. 41 Deepak Sethi/iStock /Thinkstock; pp. 44, 49 NicoElNino/Shutterstock.com; p. 46 Freedomz/Shutterstock.com; p. 51 iPhone/Alamy Stock Photo; p. 54 puhhha/Shutterstock.com; p. 58 Google screenshot, Google and the Google logo are registered trademarks of Google LLC, used with permission; p. 60 Lili White /Shutterstock.com; p. 64 Bloomberg/Getty Images; additional background textures and graphics Verticalarray/Shutterstock .com (p. 1), Toria/Shutterstock.com (p. 3).

Design: Michael Moy; Layout: Nicole Russo-Duca; Photo Researcher: Nicole DiMella